My Father on a Bicycle

My Father on a Bicycle

Patricia Clark

Michigan State University Press
East Lansing

∞ The paper used in this publication meets the minimum requirements of
ANSI/NISO Z39.48-1992 (R 1997) (Permanence of Paper).

Michigan State University Press
East Lansing, Michigan 48823-5245

Printed and bound in the United States of America.

11 10 09 08 07 06 05   1 2 3 4 5 6 7 8 9 10

LIBRARY OF CONGRESS CATALOGING-IN-PUBLICATION DATA

Clark, Patricia, 1951–
My father on a bicycle / Patricia Clark.
    p.   cm.
ISBN 0-87013-741-7 (pbk.: alk. paper)
I. Title.
PS3553.L2876M9   2005
811 .54ˉDC22   2004025620

Michigan State University Press is a member of the Green Press Initiative
and is committed to developing and encouraging ecologically responsible
publishing practices. For more information about the Green Press Initiative
and the use of recycled paper in book publishing, please visit
www.greenpressinitiative.org.

Book and cover design by Valerie Brewster, Scribe Typography

Cover art is *Bicycle Man* (1992) by Frances Hynes and is used courtesy of
the Telfair Museum of Art, Savannah, Ga.

Visit Michigan State University Press on the World Wide Web at:

www.msupress.msu.edu

In memory of my parents

―――

for Stan Krohmer

And what I would not part with I have kept.

ROBERT FROST

Contents

ONE

TWO

THREE

My Father on a Bicycle

ONE

My Father on a Bicycle

If you ever saw my father in shorts,
you wouldn't forget his stick-thin legs,
the knees knobby as windfall dwarf apples.

And the only time I saw him ride a bike,
Oakes Street, I think, he pedaled "no hands"
down the street to show me the stance.

He wasn't a runner either, though he'd move
at a quick trot when trouble came to our door—
usually when the twins caught somebody's wrath.

Once they set an oatgrass field on fire, and trucks
came, red and furious down the boulevard.
Another time, after a morning of water-fat balloons

lobbed at cars, the cops shadowed our porch.
Our father was an ambler, a stroller, a tall stander.
I can see him, heron-alert, bare-headed,

the waters of the Satsop or Nooksack, the cold
Chehalis, up past his knees, casting a line
among boulders, deadwood, and drop-offs.
Deep, moving water his abiding friend.

American Elegists

Silver meadow, the upland meadow with a path.
The field with a stand of sumac, the understory where
rabbits browse, and the field of red-tipped grass.

Full summer with the dual rising whine
of pesky flies and, up the field, a chainsaw
where workers clear trees to build a house.

Now woodland sunflowers next to yarrow, white,
take over in the sun, and purple vetch in shade
replaces dame's rocket that wafted its scent

all through the woods. I shake my head, no,
nothing elegiac in July's hot air, and yet
the robins seem to sing it at dawn and at dusk.

They group on the cool lawns, sometimes three—
sometimes one adult and two or more
immatures with spotted breasts. They run forward

a few steps, spread out wings halfway and then
stop, twist an eye down to the ground before
spearing at something, gobbling it up.

They sing only from the trees, never the ground.
I used to overlook them, longing for the fleet
hummingbird, buzzing and dazzling, or for the bright

goldfinch in yellow and black. Its looping flight
was one of its trademarks, never the song.
The robin seems to warble on the margins, slim,

of either waking or drifting off—its song part
dawn dreamscape, partly sorrow, harbinger of change,
the flowering about to come, or of the slow decline

any heart will go through, any forest or field,
the woman who has lifted many children up
now taken to rest, or nearly to that point.

In my hand I cup two halves of a round seedpod,
each a cup itself, and in one half you could drink
the bitter and in the other only the sweet, the way

I startled and then considered its color—the outside a dull,
nubbly, ordinary brown, the inside a lavender-pink wash
like the concave hidden lining of a vein, or a heart.

for my mother

Out with the Monarch, the Vole, and the Toad

To live as they do, vulnerably, in the air,
the wing-assaulting wind, to breathe
the wind, the cool September air, and watch
the *Sweet Autumn* clematis twine and climb.
To live with the scuff and smatter of leaves
at the burrow hole, the dying fall of the pink
geranium petal, the tomato stalk blackening from last
night's chill. To live with the thought, the weight — the dead
branch pitching down to shatter in the yard,
the hawk's shadow, the days ahead
without sun. A full moon spills its cream
over Dean Lake and boys at midnight
putter on their scow. An exhalation from the lake
rises to surround them, safe with a light,
though far from shore. To live with water's depth
and dark, some force that wants to pull things
in and down. To live hidden, hurrying, hurt.
The toad finds the upturned pot and crouches there,
but the snake crawls across the flagstones' warmth
and surprises it. To live the death, the thrash
in red, the awful struggle, to let breath go.
To hunker down and yet be lifted up, skin tingling,
synapses firing, the heart a-beat, awash, eyes
wide, nose lifted to what is perceptibly near.

Bumper Crop

Ping and ricochet off the flat
carport roof, they hit and bounce
on the deck's wide planks. At night,

they drop with the footfall of a live beast
onto the house, rolling toward the edge
in dreams. All September the litter of them

rained down from the tall oaks, nugget-
crack and report on wood, metal, glass.
On the house's west side, they marbled the ground

as in a comedy routine: see if you can walk here,
upright. As children, we gathered them
in kerchiefs or hats, picked up the brown

smooth ones and the green ones, capped still,
and fancied them human like us, some
tasseled, some plain, giving them names,

placing them in the fragrant Corona-box houses
under hinged lids where we closed them
at night in leaf-beds, two by two.

Or cracked them open, the way we split rocks
behind the garage, forbidden because it sometimes led
to throwing rocks—*you could put her eye out.*

A child's secret, the odd urge, to hoard them
for supper alone, closet dark, corduroy coat
with the pockets I filled, seeing myself

as a refugee running off—a story sketched
by a book, where a girl fashioned a new life
in a hollow tree she found. I still see the white meat

tinged with green in each acorn, how long
it took to dig out, fingernail or knife, what
only crumbled then in my palm,

never enough to nourish or sustain, its taste
bitter as the windfall crab-apple, the knot
of belly-ache far, far into the night.

Western Slope

A drink the color of malachite or jade, Green River
from a shaped glass, the flexible straw, long sip,
while you turned, swung, tapped your toes
under the soda fountain bar. The walk down 56th Street
to South Tacoma Avenue, allowance, coins,
the public library, five-and-dime, gone, all gone.

Fretted verdure, the splash of light through green
into the front seat, and two ways to go: up the hill, rutted,
gravelly, and church-roof steep, or the way
where branches scratched the car, and the blind
corner—Father letting you press the horn as your three
sisters screamed and covered their ears.

Water just off the shore where the bottom fell
away—emerald, verd antique, aquamarine.
And the jellyfish floated, a Medea-head, yellow-gold,
big as a cabbage, tentacled, poisonous. The boat's motor
kicked and the line snapped, pulling you up
on skis, the wake rolling toward you, something alive.

On the cliff, we balanced in wind, three figures,
four—hands in coat pockets, then arms swinging back
and up, so the coats became sails on that salt air, and down
below grew poison oak, the tangled no-path to the bay,
and we teetered there, letting the northwest gusts
buffet us, holding us there on the verge, balancing.

Coming back green, evergreen, down through clouds,
and the airplane flaps lowered with a shudder, jolt,
as though anything could slow the shock. Father dead,

the house sold, Mount Rainier a chilly constant
touched golden in late sun, the whole western slope
a glacier field that never stayed in place.

White Sweet Clover and All the Other Named and Unnamed Flowers

White campion, first, for being ubiquitous
and fetching, its puffy calyxes

like the thoraxes of bees, plump, pendant.

And another pale one—wood anemone
with its opposite leaves, deeply palmate,

above which the flowers look creamy, shy.

Field clover, red, and the white sweet one,
too. Does the metalmark find it by scent?

Fading now, almost finished for the season, the elegant

reclusive stalks of dame's rocket in three colors—
pink, white, lavender. The last has lasted

longest, color of the dusky hours, the hours

of sorrow and reflection, of missing someone dear,
of words said that cannot be taken back.

A purple twining one, relative to the sweet pea,

which is called crown vetch. It adds
nitrogen to the soil and makes a stunning

companion along the roadside. Daily you fill in

one more name on the family tree, daily a new one
blooms. Soothing, idle purposes, oh summer.

Astrid, Siggy, and Bert

Where the mop-head hydrangeas lolled pink and blue
between our house and theirs, where the pear tree
scattered its white foam outside the first-floor window

of their bedridden mother, where the rabbits escaped
our hutch and, yes, did chew every green stalk rising

in their vegetable patch, where Bert rescued
the child wailing behind a locked door from the dark
cave of the garage hung with sticky curtains

of spiders. Where one day an ambulance bumped the curb
and white-coated attendants ran to wheel out the old woman,

chrome glinting, past the improbable snowball bush,
never to return. Oh, the sweet-smelling house — yeast,
and lemon — where they lived without clutter or dust.

Oh black-and-white cat named Andy, Swedish too,
no doubt, with his four meticulous paws. If we shouted

in the streets, gusty days, doing our best to loft
paper and balsa kites flying bed-sheet strips
for tails, if Father joined us, tall as the one fir

sailing our front-yard, showing us how to unwind string
and *run, run into the wind;* if we careened into beds

of neat iris, no word of reprimand escaped their lips.
Three kind muses of the first rank who came bearing
cookies on a blue plate, they cut and mowed, pruning

an order to all that grew on the lattice of our lives—
vanished now, names nearly lost, faces watery, erased.

Inflorescence: Fennel

Airy green stalk that raises
a compound umbel, seeded
and gold, as it grows.
What footing hides,
darkly, underground?
I neglected it for weeks,
till it tipped, rain-
battered, spindly, trying
to grow sideways. Only then
did I bring out stakes
and twine. Before first
frost, I'll carry out
a spade from its hook
in the garden shed, then dig up
the striated greenish-white
root. Time, one fall
night, to prepare whole
baked trout on a bed
of Roma tomatoes, sliced
and seeded, with carrot, garlic, oil,
fennel. Its skin crackles
brown, a faint rainbow
pentimento, and aromas rise,
like prayer, into the trout's
flesh. Imagine your length
laid upon something else,
a root and stem pulled
from the ground, transformed
by a rich, thick steam.
Praise to the dark caverns
of magic, ovens of earth

and house, blending of all
things together, cuisine's
alchemy, art.

La Chanson du Rossignol

after the painting by William Adolphe Bouguereau

At first glance, a standard scene—
a girl sitting on a stone block
near the woods while a nightingale sings.
But there's something heartbreaking

caught in her face, something that speaks
of the tragedies of class, of chores
repeated until the body becomes
as worn and beaten up as a shoe.

Her face, transfixed, shines
with a solemn attention that's also
weary. What do the bird's sweet notes
have to do with her? Yes,

she'll link arms with her love
at dusk and stroll here listening
to the trilling bird, but there's no denying
economics. Her interlaced hands

are red from work and her feet,
though neatly crossed, are bare,
calloused on the soles, no doubt,
and cracked. The whiteness of her arms,

the intelligent, thoughtful face
will have to be sacrificed. Before long,
she'll be pregnant, and then
again. Isn't that part of the thought

in the face, the dark knowledge
of what lies ahead? She would seize
a chance if one were offered,
and she'd make as much of it

as possible—so say the brown eyes,
the spot of red above one cheek.
In reality, though, the painter's named
and she's not. Finding her grave—

for she's long since dead—would be
impossible. Her sole moment of fame
remains this pose, the brushstrokes
by his hand in somber hues.

Dame's Rocket

Why lament the flower
planted a year ago
at the sunny southeast
corner of the garage, now
about to bloom
for the first time?
Four petals instead of five,
Hesperis matronalis
belongs with the mustard family
(as Peterson's *Guide* claims)
and is not a phlox.
Note the slender, long,
upward-pointing seedpods.
A garden escape, it was one
she noticed on their walks,
one he suggested they try
to identify, using a botanical key.
It grew in the part-sun,
part-shade under trees,
as though it were just about
to step out for attention.
Somewhere she read, *"il faut*
souffrir pour etre belle."
By the end of the season,
missing him for good,
she's sure to turn heads.
The guide also says
it was Marie Bonaparte's favorite
flower. Once, it was hers.
This one promises blooms,
in a day, to match the bruised purple
of the sky at dusk.

When, Midsummer

Here a porthole window urges me out to trees, lawns,
here white cosmos waves near the blue
      of salvia and delphinium,
here a bench, here a green man with his face
      half-eaten by weather and rain,
here the midsummer cusp has been reached,
      prairie grasses stand taller than I am,
and I refuse to lament anything but walk, instead,
to the Skokie River and bare my skin
      to mosquitoes.

Here Queen Anne's lace with flowerheads
      big as saucers floats
among the tawny, head-high grasses,
here flies the fortunate red-wing blackbird
      shrugging its epaulets as it goes
as if to say "I do exactly what I can."
Here jewel-weed, here purple loosestrife,
      and the white kind known as gooseneck,
and bindweed which knits the ground.

Here a hot breath huffs, coming off
      the prairie.
Here the nearly bare tree where the solitary flicker
      waits, watching.
Here the tufts from purple thistles cling,
      in clumps, before they'll be blown
everywhere, sowing, germinating.
And now the hardbitten knowledge of what cannot be.
I wave my hand at it, shoo, and watch a small flock
of goldfinches startle up
      in front of me.

Only after I've turned back, do I see a path
        through green to a swaying footbridge.
Hidden in brambles until I turned around, it offers—if I
could step along that way—crossing the river
into another life. Something holds me
here, still.

If the Present

If the clock of the long now,
its gong sounding once
every thousand years,
if the red-breasted nuthatch
traversing the tree trunk, making
its repetitive hum, headfirst
down and then up,
crossed paths with a luminous
green thing called katydid
but renamed, today, transparent-
citrus-thing-angled-like-a-leaf.
If the bee nuzzling the bright
yellow blossom of a tomato plant
and then sipping at the fountain.
If the hurrying could stop
like a stone, if the vole
didn't cower and race for its den.
If the harmony, the tune
of an August afternoon—
nuthatch, bee, water bubbling over a lip
of stone. If your lips upon
mine, that tune as well.
Oak leaves ticking a new time,
water gurgling it, the heartbeat
slowing now, steady, sure.
If the present.
If, now.

Riverside Ghazal

Most watery of all the trees, these willows
stand in water. Ice pools around the ankles of willows.

A tree's name should reveal its nature.
Salix babylonica: the first word is for willow.

Doesn't it sound stretchy and pliable?
Babylonica is for the weeping part of willow.

From a quotation in Psalms: by the rivers of Babylon
we wept. The people hung harps on willows.

The weight gave them a bent, permanent shape.
A girl flings her hair down, a young willow.

A golden color, like a shout, all the length
of the fronds. They light up the willow.

Nearby on the concrete ramp, an ice-filled boat
waits for the sun to unmoor it, sail it past the willows.

In the season of thaw, this ice giving way.
By the rivers of America, we wept these willows.

Underfoot

Twisted, leathery, dark reddish-brown,
they litter the walkway and the ground

by the stand of slender trees. What are they?
Acacia, locusts? Their seedpods lie

where they have fallen — inch-wide, nearly
forearm-long, stiffened casings for seeds.

Feeling bumps along its length, I counted
twenty-two inside one. No other fall

do I remember this embarrassment of late fruit
lying everywhere underfoot, careless, rampant

for life, tripping people up as they step by,
turning redder and slick in November rain.

How many days will they contort here, some
splitting open? How many months must I endure

the brittle clicking of seeds (so many tongues!),
their forlorn rattling in the trees' bare limbs?

What's Been Feared

How forlorn in snow—the golden hairless horse
and the blue rocket ship, waiting for spring
with the merry-go-round, the tire swing. Of course,

till then they can gaze at Canada geese on the wing,
the random inland gulls, the shoreline willows.
And the blue rocket ship waits for spring,

for children to return, watches instead the pillows
of clouds skitter by ahead of the arctic chill,
the random inland gulls and weeping willows.

The playground rides stand coldly still
this time of year, bright in red, yellow, gold, blue.
Clouds skitter by ahead of the bone chill

heading east, leaving this wintry state, too—
for the children seem to have left, disappeared
in mittens and coats of red, yellow, gold and blue.

The empty swings show what's been feared—
the children seem to have left, disappeared.
How pitiful in snow—the golden hairless horse
with a merry-go-round, a tire swinging on its course.

Elegy

Four trees form a square, as though planned.
Two are plums, two are pear. The plums
fall heavily on the green canvas of the tent.
Purple plums. In the creases of canvas, earwigs
that give you bad dreams. Spiders that made you
cry out once, in the garage when the door locked.
Mother cans the pears. The full jars glow like jewels.

At the fence of many sorrows, there is no gate,
no words for what will take us over,
or through. A dark feather lies on the cool
flagstone patio. An elm tree offers
consolation. Lie down in the here and now,
or go back, back. And the street has no
sidewalks and the hill at first is not paved.

Hutch for a rabbit near the garage. His gift's
the proof that Grandfather loves you best.
You've named her Nervous. All yours. The name
for a female is *doe.* You sing in the raspberry
bushes near the hutch and pick berries. Soft,
furred on your tongue. She eats green pellets,
made of alfalfa. *Do, re, mi,* a small dance.

The other rabbit is a buck. You can't recall
its name. Grandfather again. It's the way
to make babies, so he helped Father build
a bigger hutch, roomier. Red Xs on a wall
calendar to mark when they'd come, but in her box
something chewed, something ratty. They eat
the babies if something scares them. *Why would they?*

Another litter, seven, and mostly white but some
with black markings. Now we give them names, now
we bring them to the park and sometimes dress them
in doll clothes. All the other kids want to play with us.
Though you'd been warned, someone left the hutch's
door open. Now each movement accelerates to dark
sorrow, to the ending already written.

Years later, would I understand? Years later, I still
remember the high decibel a rabbit cries out
when struck. After the first note, there were more,
and rabbits strung up from the clothesline, to bleed.
Father couldn't have done it alone; someone helped.
Feet flying, I was already in motion, one last shriek
touching a hair in my right ear before I turned
the corner, running, and was gone.

TWO

Schooling

All the mornings, September to June,
rising before you were quite awake,
all the breakfasts, all the frothy milk.

All the things carried in knapsacks, pockets, fists,
the coins for the Offering when there was church,
a maple leaf for tracing or pressing during Art,

the pencils, newly sharp, and erasers meant
to fit on the ends, some a cat-tongue pink,
some in colors—yellow, blue, green.

All the books, sweet-smelling of glue and a deeper
knowledge you hoped to drink in, opening the front
your head swam at the table of contents—

history, presidents, countries, capitals of states
to memorize. And you learned, then, that time
existed long before your birth, your name written

on the flap grew smaller and smaller, and now
the gods who were your parents (Father so tall!)
grew smaller too, your town and neighborhood

shrinking, seen as through the wrong end
of a telescope, boats and cars becoming toys.
All the afternoons watching the clock, learning

the clock, the bell, the row, the desk, the alphabet.
All the order, the hunger for it like an aching
to grow up. All the revelations, the questions,

some with no answers ("what *is* eternal fire?"),
all that you'd return for, day after day, fall
after summer — this year, fractions, next year,

European history. And you believed it never-
ending, saw it everlasting, like Seattle rain. In the rooms,
a teacher bending over a desk, sleeves dusted with chalk,

guiding your hand, showing you how to hold
a pen; another one who scolded, at times, when
you wanted to give up on algebra, its x plus y squared.

How you wanted that, too: the spark-glow in their eyes.
Studying, sleeping, you woke again, and walked the sidewalks
to school, counting the cracks, naming the trees and streets.

Mastiff

Eastern Han Dynasty, Art Institute of Chicago

If he stood near my tomb
like a persistent muse
maybe death would be the next
adventure, fabulous in its rush
away from here, the green troubled
earth that keeps me waking up,
petulant, cautious of rapture or
love, haunted by mirages and déjà vu
moments. Thick in the shoulders, his
stance is alert and courageous,
ears cocked, head and muzzle lifted
as though listening to something
in the far distance. Fashioned
from earthenware and lead, of the second
or third century, his tail curls
neatly over his back and appears
to quiver with taut excitement.
He won't run off, though, or play,
or crunch bones from an offering
hand. He's sworn to protect me.
His chest and belly are bound
with the emblems of his soldierly
rank. And as long as he stays,
eyes vivid and wide, legs braced,
good, good dog, I believe
I'll be able to sleep without fear, here
where no sunlight reaches and the close
chamber walls seem to step an inch
nearer with every heartbeat.

Turning Away from the River

In the air, a taste of what we're in for,
wet damp, sharp smudge of leaf-rot,
sniff of iron-cold, something implacable,
black. Where they've stood, knee-joint
deep, in the lagoon and also at two bends
in the river, the herons are only ghosts
now, heaving upward, the wing-span wide
as they were tall, stick legs dangling
at first as though they were swimming
in air, and then a plumb-line south.
The wind skids and ricochets off water,
sheers inland where we walk, veering us.
This year it comes: there are no happy endings.

Hiking Near Paradise

Near Paradise Pass, where the icy solitary stream
sent up vapors, I rounded a bend and my heart
thumped a beat to find him down, prone in the road,
his head pillowed on one arm where he lay
smoking. It was the only time I went off alone
with him, overnight, the firs sighing overhead
as we trudged along an old logging road. His eyes
opened, when I got close, and he simply said,
"Reach into my pocket." I never felt as shy
with him as I did then, fumbling at my father's
jacket, its lint-lined plaid pocket. A gray-brown
whiskered fieldmouse hid there, trembling and
squeaking like a bedspring. When I asked he said,
"No, you can't bring it home." Two gentle natures,
the mouse's and his, how I still think of them napping
heart-to-heart a few minutes there before I came
along. I released it away from the stream, the road,
far from any dangers I could imagine, near
a half-rotted nurse-log carpeted by moss.
It disappeared so fast that my hands never seemed
to have cupped or held it, never reached
into his pocket that long-ago day, the deserted road
impossible to find now, overgrown and lost.

Chinese Print

Over my shoulder where I sit reading
there is a house, a river, some trees.
It is most likely winter and not spring.

It is most likely the dear front face
of a loved house, perhaps a lost one.
The river clogs with chunks of ice.

The trees loom as bare as scaffolding
hugging a building. And it is dark now,
night coming down with all its shadows

and its fears. Long after I've gone to sleep,
the river ice groans and snaps,
the tree sap begins to stir, and someone

inside the house, roused from dreams,
lifts her head. What images cloud her eyes?
Most likely she needs her sleep. Already

she breathes softly again, and I want to
let her rest there, before what comes.

Flies

The photo only breaks your heart
when more details are known.
Please, forget them for now.

For now, they sit together, an old
trio: father, mother, and child.
The man wants out of this place.

His right arm rests uneasily,
fingers about to fidget, on a small
table. A bad haircut, worn boots.

The child, a boy in frilly skirts,
leans against his mother's knee.
Grandfather, Grandfather, you want

to say, and reach out to save him.
There's no saving anyone. Isn't she
pregnant again? Her left hand

crosses her lap, trying to hide
where the dress pulls tight,
buttons straining. And then you see,

on the man's suit, what look like
snags in the fabric, rough places
that caught on a fence, perhaps.

But closer, closer, you see flies
settled on him, a dozen at least.
You can't take that, either.

Shoo, shoo, you keep on saying.
Enough time, later, for maggots,
flies, the fall of earth on a box,

the fragrant sweet-smelling dirt
of Winona, the etched, unbearable stone.

The Sound of a Mother
Scolding Her Grown Daughter

Tonight the wind rises on Orcas Island, snapping lines
against masts where sailboats clatter at the docks,
and roosters crow at odd hours in voices pitched
too high, where the brightly colored mushrooms of tents
sprout among trees and blooming goatsbeard
in Moran State Park, where toads hop through the parking lot
and scare away the deer. I haven't felt this vulnerable
in years, pierced again by her sharp tongue, and tonight
I'm driving away. The color of water as it evaporates
on the highway, rising up as lost souls must, ethereal,
tendriled, is a veil I drive through at fifty-five and now,
ghostly enough myself in my gray hooded sweatshirt,
jeans, I stop along the road where I pretend to be reading
a map—but I'm hunched over, trying to stop my hands
from shaking, doing what I can to wash the taste
of her words from my mouth.

Tomboys

A word for girls who climbed trees,
        who shinnied up
    the rough bark not caring
        about skinned elbows and knees,
    who rode—too fast—on bicycles
down alleys rutted with gravel.

They refused to come in from the dark
        to their names
    called in a litany of names
        by mothers standing, almost
    forlorn, in lighted doorways.
I overheard Grandmother use the word

for me. Was it that year, or earlier,
        when I'd stood,
    summer tanned and ragged,
        slicking back my hair in the bathroom,
    imagining my face as a boy's?
Steve Kirby, Jimmy Georgia, Gregory Federighi.

In 1961, in Tacoma, what did I know
        of sexual politics?
    Grandmother was telling Mother
        I was disgraceful, a renegade.
    She recommended dresses, knitting,
less time with Father, less time outdoors.

And then, at school, Sister Gabrielle's words
        scalded my face.
    "Sit like a lady," she hissed,

and I tried to, knees together,
        not knowing what I'd done wrong.
Why were the women so angry?

I've gone back, more than once, to the school
        and the playground,
    now predictably cramped and small.
            Like a refugee in a war-torn country,
I escaped without a glance back, taking
only what I could grip in my hands, or remember.

Male/Female

He would cut into the belly
of one, at the kitchen
sink, Mother squabbling
in the background, and he'd be
up to his elbows in silver,
blood shining from the knife,
the room smelling of sweat,
boots, coffee, smoke, and though
I'd been at home
in bed the whole time, I could
see the Puyallup River, the herons
rising, cattails and redwing
blackbirds with their bottlebrush
shapes and streaks of color,
from shore to shore a thick fog,
but rolling up and off like smoke, a reel
singing as the steelhead ran
with the line, the hurry, the thrash
and splashing, feet stumbling
along the shore to keep up,
to keep the line from getting cut.
Surely this was a victory for them,
Father saying *it's a female*, then
he's pulled out the whole orange clump
to show my brothers.
Yes, he is saying, *we'll use the roe
as our next bait*, and *How about
Saturday, early?* He holds them up
in front of the window, though I was never
actually there to see it, scales smeared
on the faucet, on the hump between

the two sinks, his forearms
all silver and orange on fire. The guts
and severed head lay in a mass on
papertowels. Light glinted thick
through the raised orange
globes. *Yes, good thing this was a female.*

Missing

How can I go down to the river,
nudge the car into my usual spot, and walk?
How can I set the brake and clip the leash
onto the dog's collar?

While he's lost, how can I go on stepping
along the riverbank? The path curves, near
the lagoon, and I go with it. I count the mallards,
always in pairs, most domestic of the ducks.

He's lost somewhere in the river,
boat found, shoes and creel found, but he
himself lost between Rockford and the blue bridge
at Fulton Street. How can I go easy?

While he's lost it doesn't seem right
to walk without aim, to study swollen buds
on the willows and oaks, to long for the ground
softening, for the spears of green to come.

How can I go easy down to the river, water
where I dipped my hand after my father died,
river that I asked to soothe him,
and now the river that has taken this life?

Rivers are where my brothers stand in their tall
hipboots, lines swishing out like the lithe tongues
of frogs to nab a tasty bug, rivers where
my father stood, seeking quiet away from home.

One day a red helicopter clattered along overhead,
low and looking, and it wasn't a time to wave.
They went searching along the riverbank. It wasn't my
brother they looked for, but it might have been.

How can I go down to the river, tomorrow, today,
drive down and steer the car into a spot,
knowing that he's lost in water cold
as slate, soul seeking for a way to climb out?

Against Time

for Grace

Dated 1912, a penny stamp stuck in a corner,
the postcard from him
       to the woman he'd marry in a year
bears a message scrawled sideways
                    in pencil
and the blustery "Hello kid"
brings his voice back to me.

The flip side shows the dirt-packed
                  main street
of Baker, Montana, with shops and hitching posts
a faded gray.

A joke, perhaps? He's written, "Say,
                this is some town."
Whatever business he was on,
      if business it was
and not cards, gambling, that year
my grandfather was twenty years old.

He closes with a casual "See you soon"
      and his initials.
Say what you will about scraps
of nothing, the impossibility of knowing
      another person's heart—

still, I hear the note of affection clearly,
as clearly as I hear his voice.
      From elsewhere, too, from dusty boxes
shoved into closets, carted
      house to house, state to state,
          more notes.

Was it a kind of love to have saved
this stuff—for it's her doing—
                    saved the postcard
nearly seventy years before she died?

Or was it a reflex, blind,
instinctual, to hoard what's been dear,
to keep it, store it, not to look at,
                    but to hand on,
so someone else would read it,
would know, would remember?

Spider Among the Clementines

A pale rust-colored spider crept along the tray
as I was lunching outside on sunflower seeds
and two sweet clementines I peeled,

and it seemed as though its rusty hues
were part dirt and part sunshine of the late
August day, ripening to fall, the air

already cooling. It was through a sudden love
for the hapless spider—small as a breadcrumb,
facing winter all unaware—that I warmed back

to him, napping inside after our words about chores,
yard work. Now the day's labors were gone,
some cubes of chicken lay marinating in a bowl

for supper. Left to do—figure out a way to behold
each other in the proper light. Fall's light,
the light of a day coming apart under the white oaks.

The Face of Francisco Goya

after a self-portrait by Goya

He places his mournful face —
the turned-down, crooked mouth,
eyes that seem haunted and are yet
still bright, nose like a ship's prow aimed
into the wind — directly in front
of the artist and challenges him: make
the image last. If his life has been true,
he cannot ask for mercy.

Still, he doesn't have to be happy
about it. Eighty-two years old,
he keeps muttering to himself.

The self-portrait he sketched in red chalk
at fifty-three showed a gentleman in flattering
three-quarter view, wearing a top hat
and waistcoat, but the downturned lines
of mouth and eyes foreshadow
this face. Even as a court painter,
Goya was known for his candor.

In Madrid, 6 February 1799,
along the Calle del Desengaño, his *Caprichos*
went on sale for 320 reales, hawked in shops
next door to those selling liquor and perfume.
He included the self-portrait — not for fame,
but to say, "This darkness is the vision
I see. Disillusionment and nightmares."

Now, so many years later, he cannot doubt
what he reached for, wearing out his hands,

sore now from acid and ink, bending over a table
at his work. If he misses the raucous call
of the crow, the song sparrow's lilting notes,
or the human voice, he doesn't let on.

What's done cannot be undone—like marks
etched in cheek or brow. He dares us
to question him—the journey
not yet over—and steps past us
into the relentless dark.

Cataracts

Eyes are the first to go, just look
at hers — milky, opaque — so she
misses the bed in her morning try
to jump up and, at night, even guided
by the leash, runs into the porch screen.
If you call her for a walk,
you'd stand at the door an hour —
but if you nudge her from sleep
with a gentle toe, her favorite spot
a secure and safe corner, she leaps,
startled and panicky, as though
called back to life from the other side.
That's where she's going, you know,
and soon. At Fountain Street Church,
someone preached on "Do Cats Have Souls?"
And the answer, given the philosophical
terms, was yes. Once, we brought
the dog to church, for the Earth Day
celebration of animals, and it was eerie
and oddly beautiful to look and see
a rabbit's ears pointed alertly next to
a child's, or watch a young man bend around
to pet a woman's snake. They blessed
her then for a long life — the dog, I mean —
after we carried her to the altar.
Souls and sermons, blessings, prayers,
the fur of a loved animal, the cool dry skin
of a snake. I swear that in the past,
whenever I cried, my eyes pouring a rich
cascade, the dog's eyes watered, too,
but what could I see in such a sorry

state?—my eyes brimming wet and red,
foolish, nose dripping—and there was the dog,
lapping at my cheeks, tongue wiping me, not
empathy so much, perhaps, as the good
briny taste of salt.

No Balm

Sometimes a tree lays itself down
upon water, as this one I notice today,
an aspen, its bark stripped, leaf-bare, buoyed up
by water where it lies but not enough
to right or raise it, no balm will restore it
to life. Summer breeze, and sigh. In last night's dream,
a wounded man turned to stare at me,
one eye blackened, lips white and cracked.
"What did this to you?" I asked him.
"An air fire," is all he said. Isaiah says
surely the people are grass, and of this tree
would also say the people are leaves or chaff,
limbs or venerable bark. Offshore at the east
riverbank, an underground spring aerates
and moves water. Torn from the bank,
the fallen aspen's roots lie half submerged,
a sideways Medusa head, tangled and snarled
by the current. Under the wash of air from cars,
or when no breeze touches leaves, the river's voice
is what I hear, flowing through the stiffened roots,
making a throaty music, often a low moan.

for Forrest Armstrong 1943–2000

Oceanside

Wearing a striped shirt, she's half-
turned away as though the ocean
were calling her, and from the dark
haystack rocks in the far distance,
you'd know the place from nickel
postcards on sale everywhere.
Cannon Beach, and small hands grip
onto her, their faces not in the frame,
two children or maybe three—
not me, I think, but Christina
and probably Michael, lost once
in a midway crowd at the fair. She pays
no attention to them at all, but she's
divided—you can see something in her
eyes—between the water and waves
beyond, a ruffle of surf, and the one
behind the lens, definitely Father.
It's the most attractive shot of her
since their engagement. Her dark hair,
short, is lifted by the breeze and just enough
of her lips' pout remains to let me hear
how willful she could be—*last one
in the water's a rotten egg!*
She believed in swimming, in salt-
water, and teased anyone afraid
of its depth or pull, of the egg-yolk
jellyfish rolling there like severed
heads off the kelp-strewn beach.
Chances are, her heart valve leaked
then the way it's doing now. Chances
are, that surf she hears at night is only

partly blood or saltwater waves along
the remembered Pacific coast, and part desire
for him, seven years gone on the tide
that bears all bodies away from us and still
will bear hers on—past eighty, past any fear
alone tonight in bed—television murmur
from the next room—and up again to see
the overcast light of a summer dawn.

Western Washington, *In Petto*

It happened that we came, tired, to a clearing,
a campground somewhere in the woods,
and the year escapes me, the name of the place
maybe Tolmie Creek or Carbon River.
Then I saw how it would be, summer after summer.
World along the water, scrubbed earth where we pitched
the green canvas tent, shook earwigs out of the folds
of sleeping bags. When we woke, the shade of firs
or mountain shadow touched the light and filtered sound.
How long had we slept? No one of us wore
a watch. We couldn't tell whether we'd slept all
night and come, reborn, to another day
or whether we were still only halfway
to dusk. We didn't know east from west,
if it was moss or shade growing on the bark
of tree trunks, couldn't tell whether the warmth
radiated up from the ground or was the heat
our bodies made lying upon it. Finally Father asked
a man in the next campsite if he had
a watch. It was the only time I felt the knot loosen
between us and our place on the spinning
earth, the ground dizzy, all of us
floating on green, and though soon we'd
laugh and say, "of course, it's six,"
there were seconds and threads of long
minutes when we fell into a gap, spirals
of DNA, molecules and cells, hair follicles, teeth,
cartilage and bone in an envelope beyond
time, drifted loose in space, sweat
on our faces, drool in the slit of each
sleeper's open mouth, our hearts like traps,

our kidneys sieving impurities mote
by mote, severed from mind and word,
one primitive being, one group or lost
tribe. And later we had no words,
no time to speak of what had happened.

THREE

Spirit Bundle

On the Lake Superior shore, I constructed a vessel
to carry it, fashioned a container out of birch-bark curls,
ferns, a few leaves already turning red.
Combined all these with pitch, sweat, saliva, glue
of cobweb and dew. Inside I made a small nest
of sunflower seed shells, rugosa rose petals,
Queen Anne's lace, white campion, pine needles.
Then I laid it down — the baby ache, the grief
in the night, the hard knot wrestled free
from my chest.

If I said a few words, then, they cannot be
repeated. If I looked over my shoulder, no one stood
behind me. I pushed the bundle off the sand
where the waves caught it. It foundered a little but then
stayed upright, buoyed by water. The last I saw it,
the current pulled it south. The last I saw,
it was pulled around a point, water silver and lead,
silver and blue, but moving, moving away.

Snow-in-Summer

Low-lying, silver-leaved,
tumbled with tiny blossoms,
it does not clamor for attention
among its showy cousins
the coreopsis, delphinium,
the pink and purple stalks
of digitalis. I saw it
first on the nursery shelves,
later spilling over a rock wall
along Giddings and knew
it belonged
in my garden.
A perennial promise of coolness,
cerastium
tomentosum,
ground-
cover,
place-
keeper
in an island border.

Summer again,
century's end.
Why should anyone die
in the heat of St. Louis
without a fan,
without air, locked inside
with the temperature rising?
If there could only be
solace, coolness, ice,
crystals,

magic on the tongue.
If we could divide
seedlings, encourage
propagation, leaf-
cuttings, and rooting medium
for every household.

Healer of wounds,
balm for sore eyes
in our inner cities,
though not suitable at all
for cut flowers.
Star-shaped blooms
of inspiration, what if you
brought back the ancient rite
of sitting down
to supper—all day
people caught in the office air,
and then the escape to the garden's
redolent green,
the weeding, the plump handfuls
of vegetables.

Snow-in-summer, smallest
wave of delicate flowering.
You follow the crocus,
the delicious hyacinth, paper white
narcissus, tulips of every color.
After sea thrift, after the cold
has melted in patches:
your silver foliage, low

along the ground,
and flowers without fragrance,
return triumphant.

Invocation

I'm taking the drastic step of imploring the trees,
the forty-foot maple first and then the two
nearby copper beeches, russet-red sketches
of leaves above black branches. Next, I'll bend
a knee for Lake Annaghmakerrig and the hills
beyond, pastured or wooded. And for the fields
divided by hedgerows, by ditches, fields where
the foxes run, one last night with a magpie fledgling
trembling in its mouth. I stumbled onto a deer
frantic and caught in netting, its horns snagged,
and it threw itself round in a mad circle to be
uncaught. Affinity with a deer, who would think
it, yet I wanted it free—and myself, too.
Let us lift up, despite the rain, let us knock
and have open, the body's marrow, socket, heart.

Synchronous Fireflies

Dense enough to make a cloud, low-
lying, that drifts and lights the dark
of Tennessee fields. Cade's Cove deep
in darkness, and the sadness of mid-
summer heavy as wild honeysuckle twined
along the fence. And though the gold moon
lifts off and drifts, too, her face is lined
with a kind of sorrow, all that's lost
and cannot come again, though the cycle
repeats, relentless as the tide.
Their firing, though. Perhaps it's a sign
of small talk, bug to bug, where
to settle for the night, or where food
might be found. When it's not
together, it seems to make a pattern—
a question, pause, and answering blinks
of light. If I could blame it on the heavy air,
this weight, I wouldn't need to thrash
in sleep, as though to turn and turn
again might bring some ease.
But the landscape's a recalled one, lost
as so much else. A picnic place,
one I'll remember till I die.
Didn't our guide call it a "window,"
geologic, with earth pushed up to make
this flattened open place between hills?
Maybe their light has more to do
with courtship, or sex. I long
for a life instinctual as theirs, to arrive
somewhere laden and full, linked,
not always second-guessing every move,

eating regret for breakfast along
with milk and fruit. For surely now
it's dawn. When walls and lamp
and wood furniture take shape, I find
again the clips of memory served up—
a day, a meal eaten on grass, the sun
a friendly blaze—remain so frail
that firefly wings, or light of fireflies
in unison or not, seem sure
and permanent compared to all
I've tried to save.

House Blessing

for Jennifer Gehrt

When we say North 63rd is your street,
2122 your number, it means you'll remember
the drive home for years, how many turns.

You're the new caretaker of windowsills
and soffitts, gutters, valleys, roof and peak.
The inner workings of faucets and drains,

light fixtures, toilets and pipes, these
are yours. Do you still dream of apartment life,
with repair of a leak only a simple phone call

away? Or do you wake, troubled and sweating,
hearing the slab settling with a crack,
the house slumping a half inch lower

on one side? Imagine the months to come
when you snooze through Seattle's night—
and there's no smell of paint, no frown

of a neighbor over a rhododendron's death.
Instead, the rooms fill with voices of friends,
your parents, sister, uncles and aunts. A fire

snaps in the fireplace and eaves drip rain.
The young woman I remember with a curly head,
dancing in diapers with a headset on, now leads

the way to the tiletop table, candle-lit, and serves
a meal fragrant with oil, mustard, dill,
and wine. Tonight, we'll eat salmon from the coast

of Alaska. It has come, steaming and pink,
to a bright blue platter—and we lift a glass to it,
and to all journeys out of dark, salty water.

Another Sunlit Interior

after the painting Sunlit Interior *by Will Howe Foote*

I. *Table*

The centerpiece of blue hydrangeas floats,
turning, as the center of it all, sun
of this universe.

And now the plates, like planets.
Guests, like moons shadowing them.
A chair-back with its webbed, urn-shaped
pattern.

And the whole constellation of the dinner party

orbits itself,
spiraling.

But it hasn't begun to start
spinning.

Soon, there will be a knock at the door.

II. *Wingchair*

i.

The flowered wingchair as a form
of transportation —
: flying out of oneself
: riding into the interior — seated in a train,
        swaying
: galloping on the wind

ii.

The secluded life of the mind beckons
like a cave, and you step into
        the darkness.
The wedge of domestic comforts
        must be abandoned—
: goodbye, goodbye—I will miss you.
: hurray! I'm leaving.

III. *Curtain*

Between two rooms, that compulsory world
        of dinner guests to come
and the solitude, here, of the mind,

on the one hand, opening the door—
: greeting
: smiling
: lying

on the other: stepping out onto the pack ice, hoping
: to be cut adrift and yet not to be adrift—

hangs, for now, this curtain with its cool
promise:

Green, like a screen of trees. Cicadas racketing a whir
so you stop listening. A box inside a box,
inside the skull. A sunlit space.

To lose oneself in a book means to leave,
the way a body gives in to a lake, in summer.
Hands together, hands apart. Swimming.

Attention, devotion.

Nest

For the last few days, two purple house
finches have flown in and out,
flight twining through the white trellis-

work on the front porch. False spring,
false May with its early blooms—
narcissus, aubrietta, grape hyacinth,

johnny jump-ups with violet petals
that seem to shine like faces
from the lawn. The finches gathered

string, broken pieces of winding stem
from last year's clematis, and strands
of straw, grass, web. Before we knew it,

before we could carry the hanging plant
back in the house, they'd settled in, forming
a nest in the velvet-leaved plant that sports

delicate blue flowers. For the last few
days, it's become spring in earnest, May
turning to June, days like flowers or

water, what you can't hold before
it's gone. For a moment, before they've flown
off with their four nestlings, we pause

to admire the finches' woven flight,
their songs and joy in coming together,
the braiding of a nest in whatever places

life, or luck, gives us. And praise:
for stamens and petals of flowers, all that shines,
brief but enduring beauties, our lives and loves.

Next Door

It would be late, 10 or 11,
and there'd be a thin wail
licking through the open window
like a tongue of flame
that would be the baby
waking, needing I suppose to be fed,
and I'd put down my book
for a second and lift
my eyes, the way the dog
raises her muzzle and sniffs
sometimes when the television
shows images of wolves, the nose
up, whiskers trembling,
the sky above punched through—
like tin near light—with a few
stars. Deep inside, the needle
of pain, the jolt again of not-
to-be. The dog turns in a tight
circle two or three times,
huffs out a sigh and lies
down again, her tail a muff
for her black nose. Fenced, fixed,
domesticated—she accepts what is
without complaint. Now from next
door only the profound silence
that marks a household falling
asleep. Beyond midnight, through
the dark, I am counting up the chances,
the eggs, the accidents, I am considering
fate and whether it exists, and
tonight, I am studying the white furled

blossoms of a gladiola, the slight
shiver of lavender down each fold,
and how they stand out across the room,
catching whatever light there is.

The Journey

The room I sleep in rides the waves of leaves
through green air, where crows are black
seagulls bobbing on a crest, here, there,
and disappearing.

Through the porthole window, long
past midnight, sails my bed and me
asleep in it, out past the cowpath,
the curved brick wall,

up over the gardens with cosmos waiting
to turn their faces to the light, past
the elm and its branches that sweep
the ground, up past

the four-sided cupola. When I open
my eyes, I want to see the lakeshore
and the shoreline lights, the white
blur of the city to the south,

the dark anonymous carpet of sky.
I need the cooling influence of dark, of wide-
open, no screens or shutters, no glass,
no house or table places

to set. I want to be pulled, unthinking,
along with the moths, to the sweet-scented
white campion, to the blossom's center,
to the whole sticky heart.

Catkins

Along the walkway, a spattered glistening trail
        that goes nowhere, full of meander
                and roam, no beginning or end.

Under the oaks, past the lagoon, I cross
        two bridges on this walk—one black,
                with wooden planks, the other iron rust.

Seasonal pale or bright, the trees stay
        in place, sorrowfully leafless now,
                trunks scarred by a branch

that fell, or lightning that ripped and tore.
        Around one limb, thick as a man's
                thigh, a rope's tied and frayed.

The trees shrug off, at last, the ice
        and snow from last week's storm—
                thus their mysterious marks.

In November, a girl was murdered here.
        For nights her mother's face
                wore down the news in tears,

telling how her daughter was slow,
        how sometimes boys might tease
                or take advantage: *Deb wanted*

to be told she was pretty. Did the girl
        go along, smiling, to the boat launch?
                I smell the good gasoline scent,

boats and gear, try not to imagine
     the rest. Soon the leaves unfurl
        soothing all that's stark and, still

to come, the scattered catkins. Ripe,
     esurient structures of infinite beauty,
        each whorl a world of sex

and death, already ragged, coming apart.

The River Motet

The imp of the divine lives along the river,
democratic, among the tumbled chunks
of concrete, trees broken in half by last year's
storm, the asphalt path made smooth so the blind

can walk there and veterans from the Home
nearby. Why do you linger? To watch
the lovers bend to kiss, to see how wind
frets the water, to idle away an hour or two.

II.

Any town with a river is a good one
said a solid man I knew, one who understood
water, its riffs, mysteries, and its soul,

knew how the trout find still pools to lie
in, close together, their tails languid in a side-
        to-side motion keeping their heads
always pointed upriver. Wisdom is moving water.

III.

A summer downtown evening, stepping outside
late, the city long since emptied. A traffic light blinks,
turns red. You might be caught off guard each time—
        the O-ka-leee! of the redwinged
blackbird sounds a second or third time

before you turn your head. Musical, more punctual
than the moonrise, it devotes itself
to making a life along the water, nesting in brush
and rock near a blue bridge, and still singing.

IV.

First light or winter light, at midnight
when only streetlight glow burns on,
or in snowlight—which is like the light
within fog—and in all this long time

the river moves, sinuous, refusing to be
slowed at all, its face reflecting sky and
wind—now slate, or blue-gray-green, then
charcoal and silver, finally cast-iron dark.

V.

If you would, let the path take you down
to water, to the moving force, alive, that keeps
speaking—sometimes a whisper
only, sometimes rushing, turbulent,

and a few times nearly silenced by the heavy
dark of winter—though never for long and even
then, moving deep under ice—this
living thing, go down there, bend your knee.

Creed

I believe in one body, ligaments almighty, skin
wrapping the thankful bones, and the resurrection
of the stomach, waking to hunger each day

with dreams of basil and butter, fennel, old gouda
cheese, and wine poured like sunlight into glass.
I believe in the fretting of shadow and sun

on backyard grass, in the shedding of the oak,
in the temptation of an umbrella on the deck,
a table, a chair, and an opened book.

The ascension into light, especially after lying down
with another, causes us to sit at the right
hand of whatever spirit guides us, called *love*

by some believers. And I believe in perennials,
bark, moss instead of grass, the pollen stuck
on a stamen, the hyssop turning blue as the night.

Forked Tree

Tall enough to tower over forsythia and sweetbay,
it's been wracked and battered by storm, sheared
by wind, till only two upraised limbs stay,

and those mostly bare. Virginia creeper, that makes
itself a pest here, starts its way up come May,
by mid-summer making a pleated green dress

to join the tree's own few leaves. In October, it seems
to shout, arms up, and the news is what
it sees ahead—the bareness to come, iron chill

and cold, dead brown everything from duff
to crown. Almost forgotten, the summer night
I sat nearby on the screened porch, the cardinal

hour at the feeder, troubling over what looked like
a cloud drifting from the freeway, bearing all
the marks of a toxic thing in its ominous moves

roiling south. I wanted to set off alarms
but couldn't move arms or legs, my breath
tight in my chest. Along our tree-lined street,

the houses and people drowsed, and a door
clicked shut and locked. All it was, my poor
foolish and fearful child, was night coming on—

that's all, night's darkest feathery wing.

Grove

Growing alongside each other at the low place
        that often floods, the vulnerable spot
    where water from the lagoon slips out

to meet the river, trees grip the trapezoid
        of ground with riverwater moving
    past, sinuously, to fill the pond. Between

the curve of bank and the road, they stand
        grouped and also solitary, a gray,
    spindly lot with deeply-furrowed bark,

two dozen or so of the fast-growing cottonwoods.
        If the stories are true, of people
    being tied to trees along rivers in another

country, people who were sick in their minds,
        would the sounds here be enough
    to soothe anyone ill? Or would they need

more rapidly falling water, gallons that pour
        from pools thick with the shadows
    of pike, or water chunked and grinding

with ice? When river-sounds wash over me
        like the sounds of leaves, that blue-
    green deciduous murmur, I could lie down here

on a blanket dappled by clouds, reverting
        to childhood, or dream of last fall
    ankle deep in leaves, when I envisioned

a dress knitted together from the delta shapes
        of cottonwood leaves. Wearing it, I'd be
    the trunk of a swaying thing, half-tree,

half-woman, leaf color changing day-to-day,
        mood-to-mood, river stories of the past
    soaking into me as the moisture wicks up

into the cottonwoods, how the hardwoods were felled
        here, branded, floated down to mills or
    set afire for potash, and riverboats churned

the waters with people singing on a summer day,
        one couple clambering ashore to sit,
    then sleep, leaning against a tree-trunk.

Old photographs show the so-called river-rat men
        in vests, in hats, balancing on rafts of logs,
    or next to literal mountains of trees in piles,

horses, sleds, and men dwarfed and looking straight
        ahead, proud, somehow, that they could
    destroy so much. By 1900, all the trees

were gone. The slate water takes on a grave-
        stone gray, rushing toward the dam.
    Nearby, if you listen with care, near dusk—

you'll hear alone the kingfisher's rattling cry,
        before it plunges twenty feet straight
    down, the water parting clean as bone.

Riverwalker

For another day, I've aligned my breath with the river,
laced up my walking shoes and set out,
miraculous, really, some days believing
I could traverse the city, keep on walking,
carry my home on my shoulders, never look back.

Today the river flowed the wrong way, the water
churning and boiling, not much to be done
but stride off my sorrow and try to praise,
if I could, the good green buds swelling at twig-joints,
and fallen catkins, red and spongy underfoot.

Let me begin again as a wet thing wrapped
in hair, let me locate, finally, the triangle of a house,
another house, and then a third. Always on foot, the walk
to Visitation School, to the parish church, and the carefree
walk to the hill, a place that was mine alone.

For another day, I've given in to the spangled wet
of the river's face, to my face, and to the dog's
unfailing heart, our sixteen year alliance one
of stepping out, of sharing the bright air, of twinned
hearts, if it comes to that, bound with a leash.

A different day looms ahead, and the dog's gait,
her stumble, foreshadowed it, so slight, though,
it might have been imaginary, let it go now, and some
cooling air breathed us both into action, and we set off
again, almost forgetting, not looking back.

What is it that darkens my way, that swerves me from
the path? A shadowy warp-monster seems to stalk
my steps, keeping me niggling and spirit-small
when that isn't me. What lodges inside here opens
to embrace the riverbank verge, the fields,

and the willow cracked in half, ruined by the wind
last night. In truth, the hill never was free, or mine
alone. For another day, the compass swings wild
in its case on my jacket, the river the only landmark
to follow, its water a magnetic, quick-moving, force.

Rock School

We are the birds of the same branch. —WENDY EWALD

How many evenings, the gray shawl of dusk
wrapping the two-story house,
the sisters lined up on the porch and one
pacing in front, a lecture underway,
parental, imitative, *I'm going downtown*
to smoke my pipe, this a game
repeated, played until the words
entered bloodstream and cells, stayed
like syllables of prayer. *And if you let*
the wicked witch in, here a cold spurt
of fear, shiver of half delight because we knew

this witch, igneous rock combination blown
out of the dark, the first grade nun,
brittle as bone, and mother on a bad,
bad day, the time we knocked a whole shelf
of seedlings down, smash, dirt and green
all mixed behind the dryer. *I'll spank you*
with my old rubber shoe. Here the hand
coming down, hairbrush, spatula, anything
stiff enough to hurt, vacuum cleaner
attachment, and she screams at father,
you get out too, go, go, leave me alone.

The trick was to pick a name she didn't know,
a word or fruit she couldn't guess, or else
the witch transformed us by her spell. A girl
reads every night, pages turning like days
or leaves on a tree, looking for *huckleberry,*
quince, salmonberry, rose hips, blue rounds
of deadly nightshade. Mother to daughter, the fallen

shelf, the word made magic, the wicked witch
casting a spell to trap one forever, a turn of phrase,
motion of hand, the sister in front of us turning
on her heel, becoming Mother in front of a mirror,
or her face looking out from a photo, a voice soft,
then harsh, then deeply soft and calling my name.

ACKNOWLEDGMENTS

My thanks to the editors of the following journals or publications, in which these poems first appeared.

"My Father on a Bicycle," and "Riverside Ghazal," *The Atlantic Monthly* ("Riverside Ghazal" reprinted in *Poets Against the War*, Nation Books, 2003)

"The Bombay Laugh," "While Visiting Napa Valley, I Dream of My Brothers," and "Synchronous Fireflies," *Boolaboo*

"La Chanson du Rossignol," *For Poetry*

"Rock School," *Gulf Coast*

"Next Door," *Iris*

"Inflorescence: Fennel," *Margie*

"No Balm," "The River Motet," and "Underfoot," *Nimrod*

"Mastiff," *Poetry Magazine*

"The Sound of a Mother Scolding Her Grown Daughter," *Poetry Miscellany*

"Tongue Point," *Rhino*

"Spirit Bundle," *RUNES*

"Flies," *Sin Fronteras/Writers Without Borders*

"Male/Female," "Out with the Monarch, the Vole, and the Toad," and "Snow-in-Summer," *Slate*

"Forked Tree," "If the Present," and "The Journey," *Smartish Pace*

"Chinese Print," "Tongue Point," "Toward Home," and "White Sweet Clover and All the Other Named and Unnamed Flowers," *Stand* (England)

"Bumper Crop" and "Hiking Near Paradise," *The Texas Observer*

"Against Time" and "Tomboys," *Widener Review*

"Grove" and "Turning Away from the River," *Valparaiso Poetry Review*

Thank you to the Ragdale Foundation and to the Tyrone Guthrie Center at Annaghmakerrig (Co. Monaghan, Ireland) for time, space, and fellowship which aided in the completion of these poems. Also to ArtServe Michigan for a Creative Artist Grant in 2003 from the Michigan Council for Arts and Cultural Affairs. And to Grand Valley State University for its generous support through a sabbatical leave and travel grants.